WE WERE HERE FIRST
THE NATIVE AMERICANS

THE
BLACKFEET

Wayne L. Wilson

PURPLE TOAD
PUBLISHING

WE WERE HERE FIRST
THE NATIVE AMERICANS

Printing   1   2   3   4   5   6   7   8   9

Author's note: Technically the names *Blackfoot* and *Blackfeet* are interchangeable. *Blackfeet* is more commonly used for the group living in the United States, because that is the spelling the U.S. government used in treaties with the Native Americans. Canadian treaties used the term *Blackfoot*. According to tribal leaders and the literature, members of the tribe consider themselves all part of the same group. Members usually use their band name instead of *Blackfeet* or *Blackfoot*.

Publisher's Cataloging-in-Publication Data
Wilson, Wayne L.
  Blackfeet / written by Wayne L. Wilson.
    p. cm.
Includes bibliographic references, glossary, and index.
  ISBN 9781624693182
1. Siksika Indians—Juvenile literature. 2. Blackfeet Tribe of the Blackfeet Indian Reservation of Montana. 3. Indians of North America—Montana.
I. Series: We Were Here First: The Native Americans.
E99.S54 2017
978.00497

Library of Congress Control Number: 2016957215

eBook ISBN: 9781624693199

CONTENTS

COUNTING COUP

Grasping his coup stick, the warrior crept through the trees, inching closer to the voices. He saw three United States Calvary men standing by the river. Their horses were tied to a post. After a while, two of the men grabbed their rifles and marched along the riverbed. The third remained with the horses.

The warrior crawled stealthily through the grass toward the soldier. The soldier's hands were on his hips as he gazed at the sparkling river. The warrior easily could have killed him with his knife. Instead, he jumped up and whacked the soldier on his back with the coup stick and shoved him into the river. The warrior picked up the soldier's carbine and pointed it at him. The drenched soldier stood in waist-high water and raised his hands. He feared he was going to die as this Blackfoot warrior glared at him. The warrior slowly backed away. He used his free hand to untie the horses.

Suddenly, the warrior heard rapid footsteps headed his way. He slipped the rifle into the saddle scabbard and leaped onto the horse. He grabbed the reins of the other two horses and galloped off, whooping loudly. Hearing

the crackle of gunfire, the warrior kept his body low. He felt the heat from a bullet as it whistled past his ear.

Later, the young man rode triumphantly into the Blackfoot camp to a cheerful welcome. He had left on foot, but returned on horseback with a soldier's rifle and two additional horses. Men, women, and children gathered around the hero, eager to hear him tell about counting coup.

To "count coup," warriors performed acts of bravery against an enemy. Each coup gave him a higher status in the tribe. The word *coup* (KOO) comes from the old French trappers and traders. It means, "a blow."[1] A warrior's mission in counting coup was to get close enough to an enemy to strike or touch him without getting injured or killed. Coups such as hitting an armed enemy, capturing weapons, freeing tied horses, or stealing ceremonial pipes from an enemy's camp were given more respect and importance than killing a foe.[2]

Edward S. Curtis took this photograph, called *The Three Chiefs, Blackfoot, Montana*, on the Montana plains in 1900.

CHAPTER 1
THE BLACKFOOT CONFEDERACY

We Indians do not have written history like our white friends. Ours is handed down from generation to generation orally. In this way we have preserved our Indian history and our legends of the beginning of life. All history the Native learns by heart, and must pass it on to the little ones as they grow up. —Percy Bullchild[1]

The Blackfoot Confederacy was also called *Niitsitapi*, meaning "original people." They were one of the most powerful tribes of the Plains. Their language, Siksika, is one of the Algonquian languages. The confederation was made up of four distinct bands: The Northern Piegan (Aputsi Pikuni), Southern Piegan (Anskapi Pikuni), Blood (Kainai), and Blackfeet (Siksika). During the 1800s, the confederacy shared a close alliance with two non-Blackfoot tribes: the Sarcee (Tsuu T'ina) and Gros Ventre (A'aninin, or A'ani).[2] Before 1866, there was a fifth Blackfoot band, called Small Robes (Inaxix).

The nation has been called both Blackfoot and Blackfeet. The name was spelled differently in different treaties. In their treaty with Canada, the three northern bands were written as *Blackfoot*. In the treaty with the United States, the nation was called *Blackfeet*.

French fur traders called them *pen wa* (black foot) after seeing the blackened bottoms of their moccasins. Some believe they painted their moccasins black. Others think their shoes were naturally black from walking through the ashes of prairie fires. Some Blackfeet claim it comes from their ancient association with the buffalo, whose hooves are black. According to Blackfoot historian Jack Gladstone, "We are the people of the buffalo, Blackfoot people."[3]

The confederation controlled a large territory that ranged from the North Saskatchewan River in Canada to the headwater of the Missouri River in Montana. The territory included the foothills of the Rocky Mountains.

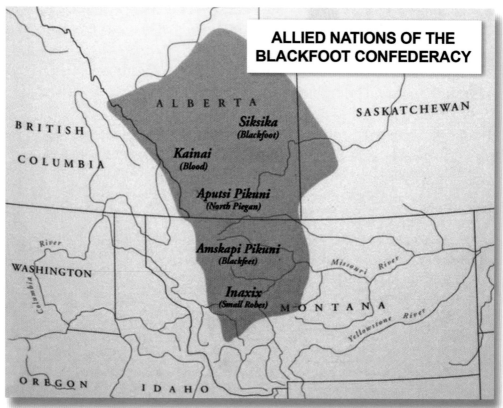

ALLIED NATIONS OF THE BLACKFOOT CONFEDERACY

BRITISH

COLUMBIA

ALBERTA

SASKATCHEWAN

Siksika (Blackfoot)

Kainai (Blood)

Aputsi Pikuni (North Piegan)

River

WASHINGTON

Amskapi Pikuni (Blackfeet)

Missouri River

Inaxix (Small Robes) MONTANA

Yellowstone River

OREGON IDAHO

The Blackfeet lived mainly in the northern plains of Montana in the United States and up through Alberta and Saskatchewan in Canada.

The Blackfeet moved their camps to follow the buffalo migration paths. When spring arrived, they hunted the buffalo that grazed on the grasslands.

The bands were nomads, following food sources as the seasons changed. They depended almost entirely on the buffalo for food, clothing, shelter, and equipment. As the buffalo moved to graze, the Blackfeet moved with them. The Blackfeet also hunted deer, elk, moose, and small game such as rabbits. They gathered fruits such as chokecherries.[4]

The Niitsitapi have a long and rich history in the Northern Plains territory. Archaeologists from the University of Alberta in Edmonton found campsites in the St. Mary River Drainage. The sites date back over 13,000 years. Blackfeet believe their people occupied the Rocky Mountain region for more than 10,000 years. "We have always been here," tribal elders state, "The people have always lived on the Plains, since the time when muskrat brought up the mud from under the waters."[5]

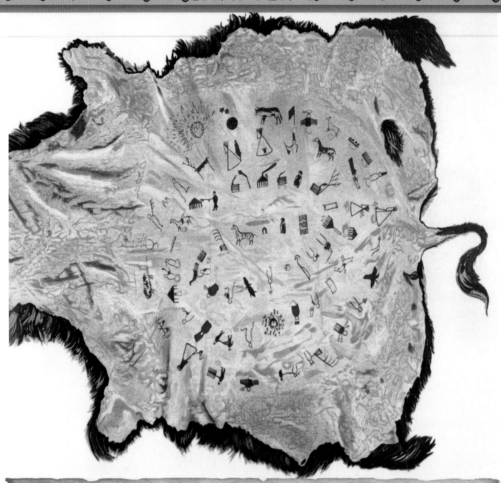

The Blackfeet and other Native Americans kept track of time by recording their tribal calendar, histories, and memorable events on tanned buffalo hides.

During the 1800s, the Blackfeet kept track of time using the "winter count." This calendar recorded one important event from each year. For example, a major storm, death, or sickness or epidemic would be recorded. Most of the time, elders memorized these winter counts. Some of them were written down later. However, at least two winter counts were kept on tanned buffalo hides. Pictures of the events were painted on the hides.[6]

Head-Smashed-In Buffalo Jump

Buffalo jumps were called *pishkun*, which means "deep blood Kettle." For thousands of years the hunters killed their prey by chasing them over a cliff. Later, every part of the animal was used for food, shelter, clothing, and tools.

The buffalo jump was used for thousands of years as a way to hunt buffalo. Hunters would drive the animals over a cliff, and then bring their kills back to camp. The Head-Smashed-In Buffalo Jump in Canada is one of the oldest, largest, and best-preserved buffalo jumps in North America. It has existed for over 6,000 years and is a very spiritual place to the Blackfoot.

According to legend, a young Blackfoot boy got too close watching the buffalo run over the cliff. His head was crushed when he fell.[7]

The Blackfoot lined up mounds of stones to keep the buffalo on a path. One hunter wore the skin of a baby buffalo. He cried like a frightened calf to lure the herd. Other hunters covered themselves in coyote or wolf pelts and waved and screamed at the herd from behind. The buffalo would stampede, pushing some members of the herd over the cliff. This was a very dangerous way to hunt. The hunter pretending to be the calf had to dive out of the way of the herd. If he didn't, he too would fall to his death.[8]

The Blackfeet called the horses *ponokamita*, or "elk dogs."

CHAPTER 2
LORDS OF THE PLAINS

BLACKFEET! No tribal name appears oftener in the history of the Northwestern plains . . . and none ever inspired more dread in white plainsmen. Hell-gate (Montana) was not so named because the water there was fiercely wild, or the mountain trail difficult, but because the way led from tranquility to trouble, to the lands of the hostile Blackfeet.—Frank B. Linderman, c. 1880[1]

During the early 1700s, the Blackfeet followed the buffalo from the open prairie during the summer to sheltering forests during the winter. They traveled by foot and used dogs to carry their goods. Some dogs were strapped to a travois (truh-VWAH), a type of sled made with two poles and a platform for the cargo.

When horses arrived on the Great Plains, Blackfoot lives were changed dramatically. Horses carried far more weight than dogs, moved faster, and could be ridden for hunting and traveling. The introduction of the horse also changed warfare.

In 1730, Shoshone on horses attacked Piegans on foot. As one historian described it, the Shoshone had turned into "centaurs nine feet tall who could dash upon their victims with

Traders brought furs and preserved bison meat to the Hudson's Bay Company. In exchange, they could receive goods such as horses, guns, blankets, whiskey, and tobacco.

the speed of the screaming wind."[2] The Blackfeet only had arrows and lances for warfare.

The Shoshone occupied much of present-day Alberta and Montana and parts of Wyoming. They continued to harass the Blackfeet. The situation changed once the Blackfeet gained horses and bought guns from the Hudson's Bay Company. During the mid-eighteenth century, fur trappers exploring westward hoped to start trading with the native people. They were the first non-Indians to visit the territory.

Although in general they did not want any settlers in their territory, the Blackfeet allowed fur companies to build forts on the upper Missouri in the heart of their country. The relationship between the Blackfeet and trading companies became very important. It brought them goods they otherwise might not have had. It also changed their lives socially.

David Thompson was a trapper who wrote a detailed record of the Blackfeet. He observed that once the Blackfeet acquired horses and firearms, by 1787, they had conquered most of the Shoshone territory. They captured many Shoshone women and children and made them a part of the tribe. Their numbers grew.

During the 1900s, the Blackfeet pushed enemies such as the Shoshone, Flathead, and Kutenai west across the Rocky Mountains. The Blackfoot

The Blackfeet were the most powerful tribe of the Northern Plains. They often battled with other tribes, such as the Sioux.

Confederation was so powerful and feared, many believe it slowed westward U.S. expansion.

The impact of the horse on the Blackfeet's way of life was enormous. Horses could move their belongings faster from one camp to another. They increased their food supply and made long journeys easier. Horses also had great trade value. The Blackfeet realized the more horses they had, the more things they could get to improve their life: a handsome war headdress, finely ornamented clothes, guns, bows and arrows, and more.

The Blackfeet also knew that their neighbors on the Great Plains—the Kutenai, Snakes, Crows, and Sioux—had many horses. Since rival tribes often competed for hunting in the grasslands, having plenty of horses was vital. Stealing horses was no longer just proof of courage, it was done to survive. The Blackfeet mastered horse thievery, and with their riding skills and marksmanship, they became known as the Lords of the Plains.

Blackfoot headdress

The Two Medicine Fight

Meriwether Lewis

In July 1806, eight Blackfeet braves came across Captain Meriwether Lewis and his party exploring the Marias River country. The meeting was friendly until Lewis explained that the United States was making treaties with the Blackfeet's neighbors. The U.S. government would give weapons and supplies to tribes that agreed to peace with the United States. The Shoshones and Nez Perce, the Blackfeet's mortal enemies, had already agreed to this peace. The government's promise to give guns to their enemies made the Blackfeet uneasy.

At dawn, the Blackfeet tried to steal the expedition's guns and horses. A scuffle broke out. Lewis shot one of the warriors, and one of his men stabbed another. One of the braves who died was only 13 years old.

The surviving Blackfeet returned to the tribe and reported on the skirmish. They also relayed America's plans for the region. The Blackfeet viewed these plans as hostile. They closed off the territory to whites for the next 80 years.[3]

Contact with the settlers and trading companies exposed the Blackfeet to horrible diseases such as cholera and smallpox.

CHAPTER 3
NO-MAN'S LAND

Our land is more valuable than your money. . . . As long as the sun shines and the waters flow, this land will be here to give life to men and animals. We cannot sell this land. It was put here by the Great Spirit and we cannot sell it because it does not belong to us.

—*Blackfoot Chief Crowfoot*[1]

The trading companies introduced the Blackfeet to horses and guns. It also exposed them to diseases.

In 1837, the crew and passengers on the American Fur Company's riverboat had been infected with smallpox. To avoid delays, the greedy captain refused to quarantine those who had been infected. Every time the boat stopped at a trading post, the disease spread to the people who traded there. The scourge swept through the Northwestern plains. The diseased boat reached Fort McKenzie, a post on the Missouri River, where the Blackfeet were encamped. Smallpox ravaged the Blackfeet community.

The American Fur Company manager saw plenty of buffalo on the plains but no hunters. Later, he found two old women chanting death songs among the bodies of hundreds of men, women, and children. Even horses and dogs died from the

A map of the Blackfeet Nation. The largest Blackfeet tribal group is in Browning, Montana.

disease.[2] Many of the young warriors who fell ill took their own lives rather than have their bodies wasted by the disease. Over 6,000 Blackfeet died in the outbreak.[3]

Still, the Blackfeet remained highly feared. They attacked and destroyed several trading posts in their territory. The stories of clashes with settlers terrified people moving west, and they demanded government protection.

The Blackfeet were not present during treaty negotiations at Fort Laramie, Wyoming, in 1851. At that meeting, the government declared all land north of the Missouri River as Blackfoot reservation. In 1855, the Blackfeet signed their first treaty with the United States. Called the Lame Bull Treaty, it ceded 26 million acres of traditional Blackfoot territory to the government.

Treaties signed in 1865 and 1868 took more Blackfoot territory. More settlers moved in. Meanwhile, the U.S. Army deliberately slaughtered buffalo herds to prevent Native Americans from continuing their Plains lifestyle. The Plains people would have to stay on the reservation. The Blackfeet and other groups became dependent on goods from the government. The food was often spoiled when they received it. Tensions soared, and the Blackfeet raided white towns for food and supplies.

One of the worst events, the Marias Massacre, occurred during the brutally cold winter of 1870. The War Department wanted to punish the Blackfeet who had killed a respected rancher. Reportedly, a member of Mountain Chief's band had committed the murder. Major Eugene Baker led an infantry to go after the entire band.

Colonel Eugene Baker, leaning on the railing at the top of the steps, with other Army officers in 1870 at Fort Ellis in Bozeman, Montana. Baker was responsible for the worst Indian massacre in Montana history.

On January 23, the infantry arrived at the wrong village. They attacked the camp of Chief Heavy Runner's band. When Chief Heavy Runner saw the men approaching, he ran to them, waving a piece of paper. The letter stated that he was "a good and peaceful man and a friend of the whites."

No one read the letter. Instead, they opened fire on him. Before it was over, 173 women, children, and old men had been murdered. (The Blackfeet counted 217 dead.) The tribe had been weakened by smallpox, and the most able-bodied men had gone out to hunt buffalo. Mountain Chief's band escaped to Canada. None of the soldiers ever faced charges.[4]

The U.S. Congress in 1874 voted to change the Niitsitapi reservation borders. No other land or compensation was given to the tribe for the land

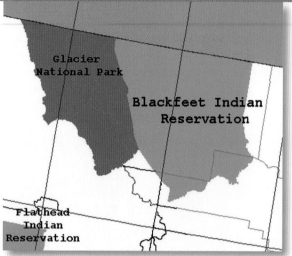

Glacier National Park

Blackfeet Indian Reservation

Flathead Indian Reservation

Glacier National Park was once part of the Blackfeet Reservation.

taken away. In 1877, Treaty 7 was signed in Canada. It established a reserve for the Four First Nations as the member bands of the original Blackfoot Confederacy.[5]

By 1879, the buffalo were nearly gone. The Blackfeet had to move to government-assigned land. During the winter of 1883–1884, no government supplies came in for the Blackfeet. More than 500 Blackfeet people died of hunger during this "Starvation Winter."

In 1895, Mountain Chief sold more land to the United States. Fifteen years later, that portion became Glacier National Park.

With the buffalo gone, the Blackfeet struggled to survive.

According to Blackfoot lore, Napi, or Old Man, created the Rocky Mountains, the Sweetgrass Hills, and other landforms in Montana and Canada. They call this beginning Time Immemorial Creation.

In 1898 the federal government outlawed tribal governments. It became a crime to practice traditional native religions. This decision was reversed in 1934. The Indian Reorganization Act of that year allowed self-government of the Indian Nations. The Blackfeet Tribal Constitution and By-Laws (1935) created a government run by elected tribal council representatives.

The Piegan, Kainai, and Siksika were pressured to give up their land and move onto Canadian reservations. The tribes became dependent upon

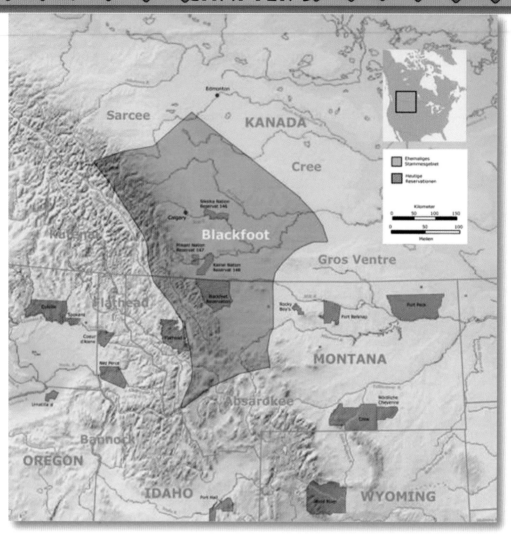

The Blackfoot Nation. The traditional territory for the Blackfoot Indians is highlighted in green. The reserves or reservations are in orange.

government food rations. They tried to become ranchers and farmers, with log cabins replacing tepees. Christian missionaries swept Blackfoot children away to boarding schools for their education. At these schools, they were forced to abandon their native culture.

Chief Crowfoot

What is life?
It is the flash of a firefly in the night.
It is the breath of a buffalo in the wintertime.
It is as the little shadow that runs across the grass and loses itself in the
  sunset.

—*Chief Crowfoot, on his deathbed*[6]

Born a Blood Indian around 1830 in Alberta, Canada, Crowfoot grew up to become one of the greatest chiefs of the Blackfoot Confederacy. He was only five years old when Crow Indians killed his father. His mother remarried. When it came time for her to live among her husband's people, she made the tough decision to leave Crowfoot with his grandfather. Early signs of his courage and determination showed when he followed his mother and new father for several hours on foot. They turned around and brought him and his grandfather with them to live among the Blackfeet.

In his teens, Crowfoot joined the older warriors in raids against enemy tribes. He proved not only his bravery, but also his leadership skills. By the time he was 20 years old, he had been in 19 battles. He had been wounded six times.

But it was not just his success in battle that earned him respect. It was also his skills as a speaker and diplomat.

Chief Crowfoot became the voice of peace and reason. He negotiated a peace agreement with the Canadian government. This wise man was called *Manistokos* (Father of the People) because of the way he cared for them.

He died of pneumonia at the age of 69.

Chief Crowfoot

Blackfeet women erect tepees as the tribe makes a new camp.

CHAPTER 4
LIFE AMONG THE BLACKFEET

Before westward expansion, the buffalo roamed the plains in massive herds. The Blackfeet relied on the buffalo for food, clothing, tools, weapons, and shelter.

During those times the main shelter for the Blackfeet was the tepee. A buffalo hide tepee housed one family of up to eight people. A leader or chief's tepee was often large enough for up to 50 people. The tepee's frame might be made of 19 pine poles, each about 18 feet long. New tepees were white, but later they turned brown. The top turned black around the hole where the smoke came out. Some tepees were painted with animals and other figures, which were often inspired by dreams. Blackfoot war tepees were often painted with battle scenes.[1]

The Blackfeet broiled, roasted, or dried buffalo meat. They stored the dried meat in rawhide pouches. When buffalo was scarce during the winters, they ate pemmican. This important food source was a mixture of ground buffalo meat, berries, and marrow grease. Deer, moose, mountain sheep, antelope, and elk were also hunted. The women added to the Blackfoot diet by gathering foods such as roots, turnips, bitterroot, berries, and the inner bark and sap of the cottonwood tree.

Blackfoot clothing was made from the skins of animals. Men dressed in leggings and often wore buckskin shirts and moccasins.

Clothing was made from buffalo, deer, elk, and antelope hides. The men wore leggings, shirts, fringed tunics, and moccasins. In the summer, men and boys often wore a breechcloth, a long rectangular piece of clothing worn between the legs and tucked over a belt so that the flaps fell down in front and behind. During cold weather, the men wrapped up in a long, warm buffalo robe. They also wore necklaces made from the claws and teeth of bears.

The Blackfeet were also known for wearing the "straight-up" headdress: a crown of eagle feathers about 12 to 14 inches long standing upright on the head.[2] Horsehair was often attached to the feathers, and white weasel tails hung down from the band. The sacred headdress was believed to protect the wearer during battle.

Women wore ankle-length, sleeveless dresses. The dresses were often decorated with beads, porcupine quills, and geometric designs. Women adorned themselves with necklaces of sweet-grass and bracelets of elk teeth, deer teeth, or seashells. They also wore leggings during cold weather.

Boys and girls played together until about the age of five. Mothers taught the girls how to gather wood, pick berries, dig roots, prepare food, tan hides, and put up and take down tepees. Fathers taught their sons how to shoot arrows, ride and guard horses, and track animals. Families held feasts when a boy killed his first animal or a girl finished her first beadwork.[3] Men could have as many wives as they could afford. Marriages were arranged by the parents, and families exchanged gifts such as horses.

The Blackfeet believe that everything related to nature has a soul or spirit, including animals, plants, trees, rivers, mountains, and rocks. They believe the Great Spirit, a supreme being, created the world. Young men might leave the camp on a vision quest. The journey lasts for several days,

The Blackfoot religion focuses on the natural or spirit world. Sun Power is viewed as the source of all power.

during which the man fasts and calls upon the gods for power. In his dreams (visions), the spirit would show him the objects he needed to collect for his sacred medicine bundle and what rituals he needed to perform. Objects might include feathers, stones, or bird's beaks.[4]

Smoking the pipe was a sacred ceremony. The Blackfeet sealed oaths and agreements this way. The host filled and lighted a stone pipe, offering its stem to the sun (father) and then to the earth (mother) before smoking it himself. The pipe was then passed to his guest on his left—honoring the path of the sun.

An antique Blackfoot stone pipe bowl. The pipe is often used in Native American religious ceremonies.

The Sun Dance, or *Okan*, is one of the most important Blackfoot ceremonies. Held every summer, it is a ceremony of prayer, sacrifice, and renewal.

The most important religious ceremony, the Sun Dance, took place in summer. The sacred vows, dancing, singing, prayer, and fasting honored the buffalo. People danced for three or four days. Dancers pierced their skin on their upper chest or back. Then they performed feats such as hanging from the ceiling of the lodge until they fainted from exhaustion or they fell. These sacred acts and sacrifices were performed to return something of themselves to nature in exchange for future benefits and good luck.[5]

Blackfeet men and women often mourned the death of their loved ones by cutting their hair and smearing white clay on their faces. After death,

The Blackfeet often wrapped their dead and placed them on platforms high in the air. These scaffolds could be 7 to 8 feet high and 10 feet long.

men and women's possessions were wrapped with their bodies in robes or hides. The bundle was left in a high place, such as a tree, so that animals would not scatter their bones. If no trees were available, they would build a high scaffold. The horses of important men were killed to provide them with transportation to the land of the dead.[6]

The Motokiks Society

Snake People Woman of the Kanai (Blood) Nation wears the ceremonial Scabby Buffalo headdress of the Motokiks Society.

In a ceremonial dance called the buffalo dance, the women imitated the actions of buffalo. The dance reminds them of a legend in which a woman marries a buffalo in order to save the tribe. It was performed by the ancient society of women called the Motokiks. At one time the society was active in all the Blackfoot nations, but more recently they performed only among the Bloods. During the buffalo dance ceremony, the group members put up a special lodge inside the camp circle. There, the women held private meetings and religious rites.[7]

The women wore ancient Notoas headdresses that they kept inside their medicine bundles all year. The headdress was based on one in the Blackfoot legend. It was made to look like a Sacred Wild Turnip Headdress. Some of the feathers in the Notoas represented the tall leaves of a turnip plant. The other feathers represented the horns of an elk. A wristlet of elk teeth was also in the bundle. Braids of sweet grass were strung on the inside of the headbands of the headdresses. The women also held sacred root digging sticks as a part of their dance. Their buffalo dance was highly regarded by all the tribe members.[8]

Entrance to the Blackfeet Indian Reservation in Northwest Montana. The Blackfeet Nation is one of the ten largest tribes in the United States.

CHAPTER 5
BLACKFOOT LIFE TODAY

The people of the Blackfoot Confederacy today live on three reserves in Canada and one in Browning, Montana. The Kainai (Blood) reserve is the largest in Canada. It relies heavily on farming grains and other crops.

The Blackfeet Reservation is on 1.5 million acres in Montana. It is the largest in the state and one of the largest in the United States. It lies next to Glacier National Park and relies on tourism. The reservation has opened a casino. It also leases tribal land to oil and natural gas companies.

Gregg Paisley lives on the Montana reservation. He explains, "Today, you find Blackfeet in all walks of life—as ranchers (many brought the buffalo back in large numbers), farmers, artists, writers, businessmen, doctors, lawyers, soldiers, scientists, and more. All are making contributions to our community and trying to protect and preserve our way of life."[1]

Paisley has started businesses to expand career choices for tribal members. One is Chief Mountain Technologies, an information technology and business services company. "I

Elouise Pepion Cobel meets with President Barack Obama in 2010. Cobel was treasurer for the Blackfeet tribe and founder of the first Native American–owned national bank. She successfully sued the U.S. Department of the Interior for taking billions of dollars from Native American trust funds. In 2010, the government approved a $3.4 billion payout. Part of the award was in land that was returned to the tribes.

am especially excited at the career paths we are opening up for tribal members," he says. "We are creating careers in a wide range of technological, scientific and professional fields."[2]

Paisley also notes greater opportunities for women. "Historically it's been a male-dominated society," he explains. "Men hunted and protected the tribe. The women broke camp, cooked, and looked after the kids. They had a very hard job. Today, there are as many women working in tribal government as men."[3]

Canada's Blackfeet are part of an organization of Treaty 7 tribes. All of the Blackfoot nations have an elected council of leaders. In 1962, the Blackfoot tribes established their own Indian Rodeo Cowboy Association, which remains a popular pastime. The tribes also host powwows to give non-Indians the chance to celebrate and learn about Blackfoot heritage.

The Blackfeet's unique language, culture, and values are being taught in schools on the reservations. In Montana, the Piegan Institute runs an immersion program. There, children from kindergarten to eighth grade are taught in their native language. No English is spoken.[4]

Blackfeet students from the Cuts Wood Academy (Piegan Institute) perform a traditional dance.

Tell us a little about yourself and your companies.

My dad grew up on the reservation, but raised a family off it. I grew up in Seattle.

I graduated from Stanford with an Master's of Business Administration (MBA) and worked in the tech industry in Silicon Valley. I retired from a long career and came back to my tribe to start operations that create jobs and put money in tribal households because of the high poverty rate.

My company is called Blackfeet Industries. We provide customer service, security and manufacturing for contracts with the Museum of the Plains Indian. I also created a nonprofit program offering programs and funding for youth living in group homes and orphanages. One project is giving kids the Christmas they might not otherwise have.

Any stories you'd like to share with us?

Today at the museum we were very busy with artists coming in and bringing their kids with them. We have a kid's table where they can color and make bracelets and things like that. We try to encourage everybody to develop their craft and get better at it.

We have nine months of winter here. If I want to buy a pair of jeans, I have to drive 125 miles. We are very isolated and in a world unto ourselves. We continue to be the people that we choose to be because our world is not diluted with much interaction from others.

What is Blackfeet life like today?

We are still struggling to claw our way back from near-extinction and one of the rawest deals any group of humans ever forced on any other group. But, we know where we must go and what we must do to get there. And we are doing it!

Gregg Paisley

Gregg Paisley: "There are 562 tribes in the U.S. and about 321 reservations, but only six are on their ancestral lands and the Blackfeet are one of them. The Blackfeet are a buffalo tribe and that means you chase the buffalo. Buffalo provide your food and clothing. You live in tepees, you break camp, and you move quickly because you're following the herd. But you do have a homeland and summer and winter camps. We were the best horsemen and called the Lords of the Plains. All buffalo tribes were warrior tribes, but the Blackfeet were the greatest raiders."

English	Blackfeet
Beaver	Ksisk-staki
Buffalo	Iinnii
Buffalo Jump	Pis-skaan
One	Ni't
Dog	Imitaa
Eat	Áóoyiwa
Hello	Oki
Indian Agent	Kinnonna
Man	Nínaa(wa)
Moon	Ko'komíki´somma
Old Man	Napi (also known as the Creator of the Blackfoot tribe)
Elk	Ponoka
Sing	Ainihkiwa
Sun	Ki sómma
Spirit Beings	Naa-to-yi-ta-piiksi
Thunder	Ksiistsi-komm
Tepee	Niitoy-yiss
White Man	Napikowann
Winter	Sstoyii
Woman	Aakíí(wa)

- In the past, Blackfeet avoided eating fish or using canoes. They believed that rivers and lakes held special powers because Underwater People called the Suyitapis lived there. Even today many Blackfeet descendants refuse to eat fish, though their lakes and rivers are filled with trout.

- War paint gave warriors a menacing and ferocious presence. The designs and colors symbolized things such as war, blood, success, power, and strength. Its magic would protect the warrior in battle.

- Blackfoot mothers carried their babies in cradleboards, a practice many American mothers have adopted today.

- Blackfoot artists are highly known and respected for their outstanding quilt embroidery and beadwork designs.

- Few Blackfoot men married before the age of 21. After the wedding, the new couple lived in either their own hut or with the husband's family.

- Frances Densmore was a famous American anthropologist and music teacher. She made it her lifetime goal to transcribe and document Native American music to help preserve their culture. One of her most famous recording sessions was with the Blackfoot leader Mountain Chief in 1916.

- The beaver is considered one of the most revered animals by the Blackfeet. The beaver medicine bundle is the most powerful. The beaver is one of the original animals in the creation story and sacred because of its role in the water.

- Although each of the four tribes is independent, they share one official language called Algonquian. It is also spoken by various other tribes in the United States.

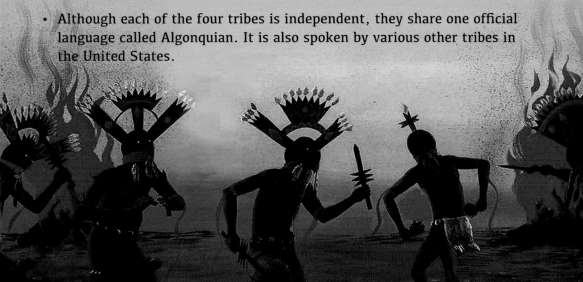

1700s	Horses arrive on the Great Plains. Blackfeet lives are dramatically changed.
1806	The Blackfeet meet Meriwether Lewis, who is on his expedition to the Pacific Ocean.
1837	A riverboat brings smallpox to trading post Fort McKenzie. Thousands of Blackfeet die in the epidemic.
1851	The Fort Laramie Treaty is signed. The U.S. government declares all land north of the Missouri River is Blackfoot reservation.
1855	The Blackfeet sign the Lame Bull Treaty. They lose 26 million acres to the U.S. government in this deal.
1862	The Blackfoot population has fallen to 6,750 people, down from 15,000.
1866	Another smallpox epidemic nearly wipes out the fifth Blackfoot band, the Small Robes (Inaxix). The rest of the band is massacred.
1870	In the Marias Massacre, U.S. forces led by Major Eugene Baker slaughter around 200 women, children, and old men. Chief Heavy Runner is among those slain.
1874	Congress votes to change the Niitsitapi reservation borders.
1877	Treaty 7 in Canada establishes the Four First Nations as the member bands of the original Blackfoot Confederacy.
1883–1884	With none of the promised supplies coming in, Blackfeet on the reservation face Starvation Winter.
1895	The Blackfeet give the United States the land that will become Glacier National Park.
1898	The U.S. government abolishes tribal governments.
1934	The Indian Reorganization Act allows tribes to govern themselves again.
1935	The Blackfeet Tribal Constitution and By-Laws are adopted.
1962	The Blackfoot tribes establish their Indian Rodeo Cowboy Association.
2009	The Blackfeet Nation creates Chief Mountain Technologies. The company aims to provide careers for Blackfeet members.
2010	After Blackfoot member Elouise Pepion Cobel sued the U.S. Department of the Interior for taking land and money from Native Americans, President Barack Obama signs the Claims Resolution Act. The tribes receive $3.4 billion from the government, including land that had rightfully belonged to them.
2016	The Obama administration cancels oil and gas leases on the Badger-Two Medicine area of Montana. This sacred ground is the site of the Blackfeet's creation story, Time Immemorial Creation.

Introduction: Counting Coup
1. George Bird Grinnell, *Blackfoot Lodge Tales: The Story of a Prairie People* (South Yarra, Victoria Australia: Leopold Classic Library, 2016), p. 245.
2. Dennis Gaffney, "Counting Coups (Counting What?)" *PBS* http://www.pbs.org/wgbh/roadshow/fts/bismarck_200504A35.html

Chapter One: The Blackfoot Confederacy
1. Narcisse Blood, "Since Time Immemorial," TrailTribes.org http://trailtribes.org/greatfalls/since-time-immemorial.htm
2. Anton Treuer, *Atlas of Indian Nations* (Washington, D.C.: National Geographic, 2014), p. 149.
3. Jack McNeel, "10 Things You Should Know about the Blackfeet Nation," *Indian Country*, November 19, 2015 http://indiancountrytodaymedianetwork.com/2015/11/19/10-things-you-should-know-about-blackfeet-nation-162477
4. Treur, p. 149.
5. Ojibwa, "Niitsitapi, the Blackfoot People" *Native American Netroots*, http://nativeamericannetroots.net/diary/1379
6. Narcisse Blood, "Since Time Immemorial," http://trailtribes.org/greatfalls/since-time-immemorial.htm
7. Ojibwa, "Head-Smashed-In Buffalo Jump Interpretive Centre," *Native American Netroots*, http://nativeamericannetroots.net/diary/1380
8. Eric A. Powell, "The Buffalo Chasers" *Archaeology*, October 14, 2014, http://www.archaeology.org/issues/155-1411/letter-from/2587-letter-from-montana-buffalo-jumps

Chapter Two: Lords of the Plains
1. Frank Bird Linderman, *Out Of The North: A Brief Historical Sketch Of The Blackfeet Indian Tribe* (Whitefish, MT: Literary Licensing, LLC, 2011), p. 9.
2. William Brandon, *The Rise and Fall of North American Indians: From Prehistory through Geronimo* (Lanham, MD: A Roberts Rinehart Book, 2003), p. 414.
3. "Untelling the Big Lie: The Murder of Two Blackfeet by Lewis and Clark Party," *Indian Country Today*, July 27, 2013, http://indiancountrytodaymedianetwork.com/2013/07/27/today-1806-lewis-shoots-indian-forever-changing-attitudes-150590

Chapter Three: No-Man's Land
1. Sharon O'Brien, *American Indian Tribal Governments* (Norman: University of Oklahoma, 1989), p. 70.

2. Ojibwa, "Smallpox on the Upper Missouri in 1837," Native American Netroots, http://nativeamericannetroots.net/diary/1604
3. Frank Bird Linderman, *Out Of The North: A Brief Historical Sketch Of The Blackfeet Indian Tribe* (Whitefish, MT: Literary Licensing, LLC, 2011), p. 14.
4. Gail Schontzler, "Blackfeet Remember Montana's Greatest Indian Massacre" http://www.bozemandailychronicle.com/news/sunday/blackfeet-remember-montana-s-greatest-indian-massacre/article_daca1094-4484-11e1-918e-001871e3ce6c.html
5. Anton Treuer, *Atlas of Indian Nations* (Washington, D.C.: National Geographic, 2014), p. 150.
6. "Crowfoot (Isapo-Muxika)" Mary's Genealogy Treasures, http://www.telusplanet.net/public/mtoll/crow.htm

Chapter Four: Life Among the Blackfeet
1. Adolf Hungry Wolf, *The Tipi: Traditional American Shelter* (Summertown, Tenn.: Native Voices, 2006), p. 127.
2. Michael G. Johnson & Bill Yenne, *Arts & Crafts Of The Native American Tribes* Buffalo: Firefly Books, 2011), pp. 133–34.
3. Ibid., pp. 114–115.
4. TrailTribes.org, "All My Relations," http://trailtribes.org/greatfalls/all-my-relations.htm
5. Ibid.
6. Snow Owl, "The Blackfoot Nation," *Native American People/Tribes*, September 2004, http://www.snowwowl.com/peopleblackfoot.html
7. Beverly Hungry Wolf, *The Ways of My Grandmothers* (New York: Quill, 1982), pp. 131–132.
8. Adolf Hungry Wolf, *Blackfoot Papers: Volume Two, Pikunni Ceremonial Life* (Skookumchuck, B.C. 2006), pp. 514–515.

Chapter Five: Blackfoot Life Today
1. Author's interview with Gregg Paisley, July 29, 2016.
2. "Blackfeet Nation Creates New Venture," *Indian Country Today*, October 26, 2009, http://indiancountrytodaymedianetwork.com/2009/10/26/blackfeet-nation-creates-new-venture-83116
3. Author's interview.
4. The Piegan Institute: Cut Woods Academy, http://www.pieganinstitute.org/cutswoodacademy.html
5. Author's interview.

Books

Blackfoot Gallery Committee. *The Story of the Blackfoot People: Nitsitapiisinni*. Buffalo: Firefly Books, 2013.

Dreaming in Indian: Contemporary Native American Voices. Toronto: Annick Press, 2014.

Dwyer, Helen, and Mary Stout. *Blackfoot History and Culture*. New York: Gareth Stevens, 2012.

Lacey, Theresa Jensen. *The History & Culture of Native Americans*. New York: Chelsea House Publishers, 2011.

Thompson, Sally. *People Before the Park: The Kootenai and Blackfeet before Glacier National Park*. Helena: Montana Historical Society Press, 2015.

Tipi: Heritage of the Great Plains. Seattle: University of Washington Press, 2015.

Wissler, Clark, and Alice Beck Kehoe. *Amskapi Pikuni: The Blackfeet People*. Albany: University of New York Press, 2013.

Works Consulted

This book is based on author interviews with Blackfeet Tribal Member and Businessman Gregg Paisley, conducted July 29, 2016, and on the following sources:

Brandon, William. *The Rise and Fall of North American Indians: From Prehistory through Geronimo*. Lanham, MD: A Roberts Rinehart Book, 2003.

Grinnell, George Bird. *Blackfoot Lodge Tales: The Story of a Prairie People*. South Yarra, Victoria, Australia: Leopold Classic Library, 2016.

Hungry Wolf, Adolf. *Blackfoot Papers: Volume Two, Pikunni Ceremonial Life*. Skookumchuk, BC: The Good Medicine Cultural Foundation, 2006.

Hungry Wolf, Adolf. *The Tipi: Traditional American Shelter*. Summertown, TN: Native Voices, 2006.

Hungry Wolf, Beverly. *The Ways of My Grandmothers*. New York: Quill, 1982.

Johnson, Michael G. *Native Tribes of North America*. Buffalo: Firefly Books, 2014.

Johnson, Michael G., and Bill Yenne. *Arts & Crafts of the Native American Tribes,* Buffalo: Firefly Books, 2011.

Linderman, Frank Bird. *Out Of The North: A Brief Historical Sketch Of The Blackfeet Indian Tribe*. Literary Licensing, LLC, 2011.

Treuer, Anton. *Atlas of Indian Nations*. Washington, D.C.: National Geographic, 2014.

On the Internet

Blackfoot Indian Fact Sheet:
http://www.bigorrin.org/blackfoot_kids.htm

Blackfoot Indians
http://www.indians.org/articles/blackfoot-indians.html

Blackfoot Names
http://www.warpaths2peacepipes.com/native-american-indian-names/blackfoot-names.htm

Facts About the Blackfeet
http://castle.eiu.edu/wow/classes/sp06/blkfacts.html

Montana Kids: "Blackfeet Indians"
http://montanakids.com/history_and_prehistory/indian_reservations/blackfeet.htm

archaeology (ar-kee-AH-luh-jee)—The scientific study of things left behind (such as pottery or arrowheads) that show how people lived in the past.

carbine (KAR-byn)—A short light rifle.

casino (kuh-SEE-noh)—A place in which gambling is the main business.

cede (SEED)—To give up control of something to another person, group, or government.

centaur (SEN-tar)—A creature in Greek mythology that was part human and part horse.

confederacy (kun-FED-ruh-see)—A group of people, countries, or organization that join together in some type of activity or effort.

counting coup (KOWN-ting KOO)—An act of bravery against an enemy, such as touching him or tapping him with a coup stick or stealing horses, and escaping unharmed.

coup stick (KOO stik)—A long willowy rod, sometimes with an eagle feather at the end, used for counting coup.

diplomat (DIH-ploh-mat)—A person who represents his or her country's government in a foreign country.

epidemic (ep-ih-DEM-ik)—The fast spread of a disease that infects a large number of people.

expedition (ek-speh-DIH-shun)—A journey made by a group of people for a specific purpose, such as to explore an area or to do research.

immersion (ih-MER-shun)—Going in completely; being completely surrounded by something.

migration (my-GRAY-shun)—Moving from one area to another at different times of the year.

ornament (OR-nuh-ment)—A fancy piece that is worn or displayed as decoration, such as jewelry or fringe.

quarantine (KWAR-en-teen)—To separate a sick person or animal in order to keep disease from spreading.

scourge (SKORJ)—Something that causes a great amount of trouble and suffering.

MEET THE
AUTHOR

Wayne L. Wilson is a novelist and screenwriter, and he has written numerous biographical and historical books for children and young adults. He is the author of the acclaimed children's book *Kate the Ghost Dog: Coping With the Death of a Pet*. He received his Master of Arts in Education from UCLA. He lives in California.